Wonders of the World

Sahara Desert

The World's Largest Desert

Megan Lappi

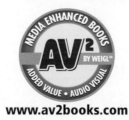

www.av2books.com

AV² provides enriched content that supplements and complements this book. Weigl's AV² books strive to create inspired learning and engage young minds in a total learning experience.

Your AV² Media Enhanced books come alive with...

Audio
Listen to sections of the book read aloud.

Key Words
Study vocabulary, and complete a matching word activity.

Video
Watch informative video clips.

Quizzes
Test your knowledge.

Embedded Weblinks
Gain additional information for research.

Slide Show
View images and captions, and prepare a presentation.

Try This!
Complete activities and hands-on experiments.

... and much, much more!

Go to **www.av2books.com**, and enter this book's unique code.

BOOK CODE

Q886435

AV² by Weigl brings you media enhanced books that support active learning.

Published by AV² by Weigl
350 5th Avenue, 59th Floor
New York, NY 10118
Website: www.av2books.com   www.weigl.com

Library of Congress Cataloging-in-Publication Data

Lappi, Megan.
Sahara Desert / Megan Lappi.
     p. cm. — (Wonders of the world)
Includes index.
ISBN 978-1-62127-477-3 (hardcover : alk. paper) — ISBN 978-1-62127-483-4 (softcover : alk. paper)
1. Sahara—Juvenile literature. I. Title. II. Series: Wonders of the world (AV² by Weigl)
DT334.L36 2013
916.6—dc23

                              2012040452

Printed in the United States of America in North Mankato, Minnesota
1 2 3 4 5 6 7 8 9 17 16 15 14 13 12

122012
WEP301112

Editor Heather Kissock
Design Mandy Christiansen

Every reasonable effort has been made to trace ownership and to obtain permission to reprint copyright material. The publishers would be pleased to have any errors or omissions brought to their attention so that they may be corrected in subsequent printings.

Photo Credits
Weigl acknowledges Getty Images as its primary photo supplier for this title.

Contents

The Great Sahara

Rolling waves of sand stretch across the Sahara Desert to create a barren, but beautiful, land. The Sahara Desert is the largest desert in the world. It is found in the northern part of Africa. All of the land south of the Sahara is called Sub-Saharan Africa.

About 2.5 million people call the Sahara home. The dry **climate** brings many challenges to the people, plants, and animals living there. They have had to **adapt** to their environment in order to survive.

Camels can survive four to seven days without drinking water. This is a useful ability when living in the hot, dry desert.

Date palms grow in many parts of the Sahara Desert. These trees produce dates, a small, sweet fruit used in baking and beverages.

Sahara Desert Facts

- The Sahara is 3.5 million square miles (9.1 million square kilometers) in size. It is so large that the entire continental United States could fit inside of it.

- *Sahara* means "desert" in Arabic.

- Only 15 percent of the Sahara Desert is covered by sand dunes.

- The Sahara is one of the hottest places on the planet. The world's hottest recorded temperature is 136° Fahrenheit (58° Celsius). It was recorded at Azizia, Libya, in September 1922.

- Most people who live in the desert are nomads. Nomads are people who move from place to place.

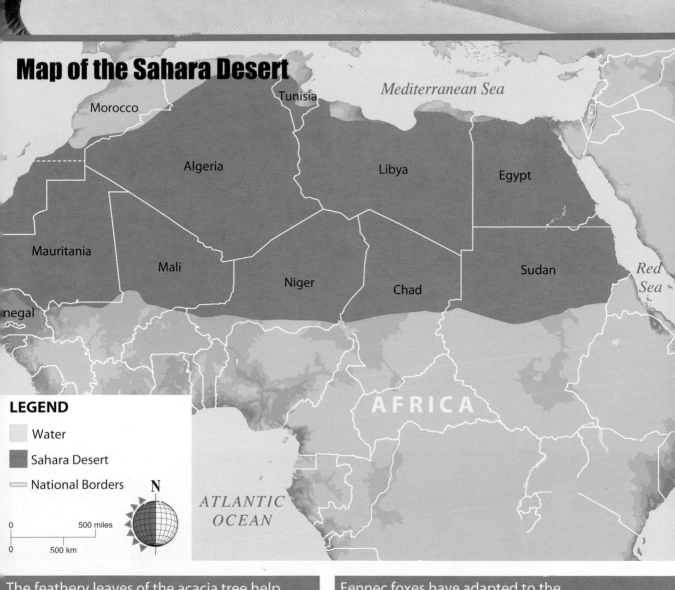

Map of the Sahara Desert

Morocco

Tunisia

Mediterranean Sea

Algeria

Libya

Egypt

Mauritania

Mali

Niger

Chad

Sudan

Red Sea

negal

AFRICA

LEGEND

Water

Sahara Desert

National Borders

N

ATLANTIC OCEAN

0   500 miles

0   500 km

The feathery leaves of the acacia tree help protect the tree's bark from dry winds in the Sahara Desert.

Fennec foxes have adapted to the temperatures of the Sahara. They release their body heat through their large ears. This helps them stay cool.

Where in the World?

The Sahara Desert covers most of northern Africa. It is bordered by the Atlantic Ocean on the west and the Sudan on the south. To the north are the Atlas Mountains and the Mediterranean Sea. Egypt and the Red Sea lie to the east of the desert.

The feathers of the desert lark match the color of the desert soil. This allows the lark to blend in with its surroundings.

Inside the Sahara are smaller deserts, including the Tenere and the Libyan Deserts. The area also has a few mountain chains. The Hoggar, the Air, and the Tibesti Mountains are all found in the central part of the desert. Mount Koussi is the highest peak in the Sahara. It is 11,204 feet (3,415 meters) high and is found in the Tibesti Mountains. The lowest point in the Sahara is the Qattarra Depression in Egypt. It is 436 feet (133 m) below sea level.

The Hoggar Mountains are found in southern Algeria. Some of the Sahara's highest peaks are found in this mountain range.

Puzzler

The Sahara is so large that it extends across 11 African countries.

Q: Identify each of the countries on the map below.

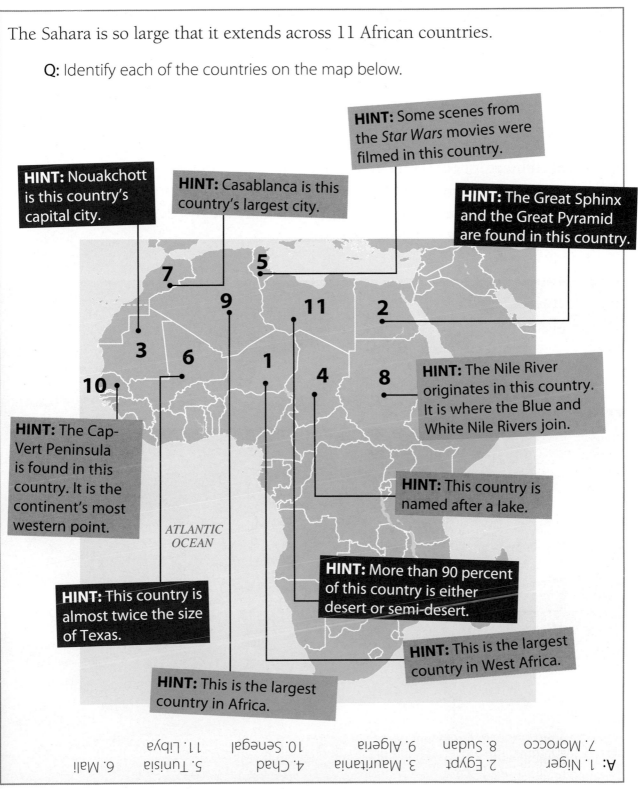

HINT: Some scenes from the *Star Wars* movies were filmed in this country.

HINT: Nouakchott is this country's capital city.

HINT: Casablanca is this country's largest city.

HINT: The Great Sphinx and the Great Pyramid are found in this country.

HINT: The Cap-Vert Peninsula is found in this country. It is the continent's most western point.

HINT: The Nile River originates in this country. It is where the Blue and White Nile Rivers join.

HINT: This country is named after a lake.

HINT: This country is almost twice the size of Texas.

HINT: More than 90 percent of this country is either desert or semi-desert.

HINT: This is the largest country in West Africa.

HINT: This is the largest country in Africa.

ATLANTIC OCEAN

A: 1. Niger   2. Egypt   3. Mauritania   4. Chad   5. Tunisia   6. Mali
7. Morocco   8. Sudan   9. Algeria   10. Senegal   11. Libya

A Trip Back in Time

Just a few thousand years ago, the Sahara was a very different place. The area had a moist climate. Grasslands and forests covered much of the land. Some scientists think that a major change happened to the climate about 4,000 years ago. Over a span of about 300 years, the area likely changed from a grassland to a desert.

In the Sahara, **archaeologists** have found **fossils** of giraffes, elephants, and water animals, such as crocodiles and fish. These animals do not live in the area now because there is too little water. Archaeologists have also found rock paintings of people fishing. These discoveries suggest that the climate was once very different.

Trilobites are a type of extinct marine animal. The discovery of trilobite fossils in certain regions of the Sahara suggests that the area was once covered in water.

Anatomy of a Desert

There are two types of deserts—hot deserts and cold deserts. Hot deserts receive **precipitation** in the form of rain. Cold deserts are covered with snow and ice.

The Sahara is a hot desert. Much of the Sahara's surface is made up of the following features:

Sand Dunes Sand dunes are hills or ridges created by sand deposits. A sand dune can be less than 3 feet (1 m) high, or taller than 500 feet (152 m).

Hamadas Hamadas are stone **plateaus** that can rise to more than 11,000 feet (3,350 m). The Atlas Mountains are examples of hamadas.

Regs Regs make up 70 percent of the Sahara's total area. They are made up of sand mixed with red, white, and black gravel.

Wadis Wadis are dry riverbeds that come to life when it rains. Most of the Sahara's trees and bushes are found in these areas.

The Desert Climate

The Sahara's climate is extreme. During the day, it is very hot. Temperatures can be as high as 122°F (50°C). Overnight, it gets very cold—sometimes below freezing. A temperature range of 86°F (30°C) from day to night is not unusual.

The desert is also severely dry. Certain areas on the edges of the Sahara receive a mere 10 inches (25 centimeters) of rain in a year. In the driest areas, located in the center of the desert, there is less rain—up to 5 inches (13 cm) per year. When it does rain, it often is a heavy downpour.

Scientists believe that it took thousands of years for the Sahara to become the dry desert it is today.

Trade Winds

The Sahara is located in the "trade winds belt." This is an area located between the **latitudes** of 30°N and 30°S.

A trade wind is a strong, steady wind that blows toward the **equator**. As the air moves from an area of high pressure into an area of low pressure, the winds become warmer and drier. This hot wind can blow for many days. It carries with it large amounts of dust and sand, making it impossible to see anything.

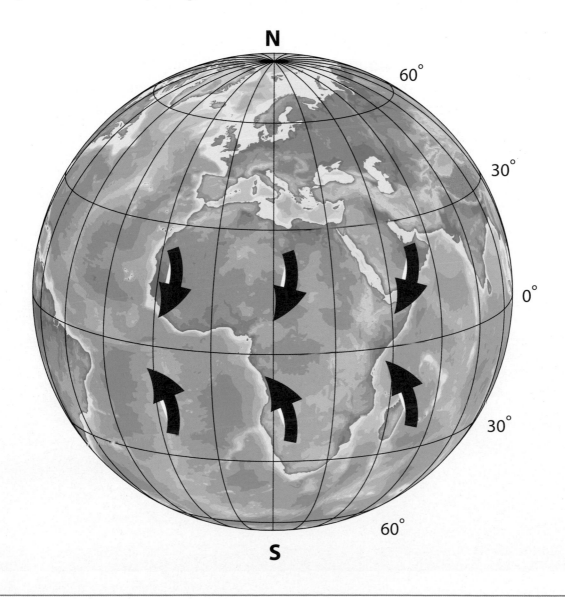

Life in the Desert

Even though the Sahara has a dry climate, plants do grow there. Patches of grass are scattered throughout the desert. The highland areas are home to several types of shrubs and trees, including cypress and olive. Herbs, such as thyme, also grow in the Sahara.

The Sahara is rich in animal life. **Mammals** found in the desert include the dorcas gazelle, spotted hyena, desert hedgehog, and Cape hare. **Reptiles**, such as lizards and snakes, live near the Sahara's few lakes and ponds. Snails, shrimp, and other **crustaceans** are found in the water.

More than 300 species of **migratory** birds, including the osprey and the sedge warbler, cross over the Sahara at certain times of year. Other birds common to the Sahara include desert sparrows, sand larks, and the trumpeter finch.

The dorcas gazelle can live its entire life without drinking water. It receives all the moisture it needs from the plants it eats.

How They Survive

Lizards are cold-blooded, meaning their body temperature changes depending on the temperature of their environment. To stay cool in the Sahara, they burrow under the sand. To warm up, they move into the sunlight.

There is a surprising amount of life in the desert. The plants and animals that survive there have adapted to living in a place that is hot much of the time and receives little rain.

Many of the plants in the Sahara live for only a few days. Their seeds then lie in the ground until the next rainfall, when the cycle begins again. Other plants have long roots that reach deep into the ground for water.

Many of the animals living in the Sahara are nocturnal. This means they are most active at night, when the air is cooler. Some animals are also able to store water in their bodies for long periods of time.

Early Explorers

The Sahara has interested many people throughout history. The Romans explored the area in a series of **expeditions** between 19 BC and AD 86. There are records of the **Berbers** crossing the desert in the fifth century.

European exploration of the Sahara occurred mainly during the 18th and 19th centuries. In 1795, Mungo Park, a doctor from Scotland, began a journey to find the source of the Niger River. This first attempt was not successful. However, Park was able to record his findings and provide descriptions of the area. He returned to the Niger a few years later. On this voyage, Park drowned while trying to escape from locals who attacked his boat.

Friedrich Hornemann was another explorer who traveled the Sahara. In 1798, he joined a caravan heading across the northeastern Sahara. Hornemann became the first European to cross this part of the desert. His journal was published in 1802. It contained little-known information about this part of the Sahara.

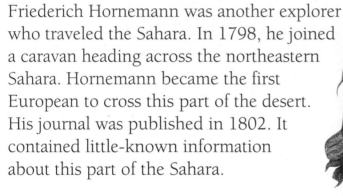

Alexander Gordon Laing was the first European to reach the city of Timbuktu, in the country of Mali. He arrived in 1826, but died on the return trip.

Mungo Park wrote a book about his adventures called *Travels in the Interior Districts of Africa*. The book quickly became a bestseller.

Biography

René-Auguste Caillié (1799–1838)

René-Auguste Caillié was born into a very poor family in France in 1799. He was inspired by the seafaring adventures of Robinson Crusoe, a character in a novel by Daniel Defoe. At the age of 16, Caillié took a job as a servant on a boat heading to Senegal.

In 1824, the Geographical Society of Paris announced a prize for the first European to come back alive from the city of Timbuktu. Caillié began to prepare for this journey by learning Arabic and studying the religion of Islam. Three years later, Caillié disguised himself as a pilgrim and joined a caravan heading to the city. He arrived there several months later.

Upon his return to France, Caillié was awarded the Geographical Society's prize of 10,000 francs. He later wrote a book about his travels, but did not continue his explorations. He lived in France until he died in 1838.

The Big Picture

Large deserts are found all over the world. This map shows where some of the world's major deserts are located.

NORTH AMERICA

ATLANTIC OCEAN

EQUATOR

PACIFIC OCEAN

SOUTH AMERICA

SOUTHE OCEAN

Sahara Desert
3.5 million sq. miles
(9.1 million sq. km)

Patagonian Desert
260,000 sq. miles
(673,000 sq. km)

LEGEND

 Desert

Ocean

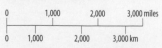 River

Scale at Equator

0		1,000	2,000	3,000 miles
0	1,000	2,000	3,000 km	

Arabian Desert
1 million sq. miles
(2.6 million sq. km)

Gobi Desert
500,000 sq. miles
(1.3 million sq. km)

ASIA

AFRICA

PACIFIC
OCEAN

EQUATOR

INDIAN
OCEAN

AUSTRALIA

Kalahari Desert
220,000 sq. miles
(570,000 sq. km)

Great Victoria Desert
250,000 sq. miles
(647,000 sq. km)

SOUTHERN
OCEAN

ANTARCTICA

People of the Desert

Most of the people who live in the Sahara Desert are **nomads**. The Tuareg and the Sahrawi are just two of the best-known groups living in the Sahara Desert. The Tuareg are also known as the "blue men" because of the blue robes they wear. The blue dye used to color the fabric often rubs off on the skin of the Tuareg, making them appear blue. The Tuareg live mainly in Algeria, Mali, Libya, and Niger. They live in rural areas, where they raise cows and sheep.

The Sahrawi have lived in the Sahara for at least 1,000 years. They are found mostly in the western part of the desert. In Arabic, *sahrawi* means "of the Sahara."

The Tuareg first appeared in the Sahara during the seventh century. They helped move trade goods, such as salt and gold, across the desert, and became known as highly skilled camel riders.

Camels

Camels store fat on their backs, creating a hump. They use this fat as a source of nutrition when food is scarce.

The people of the Sahara rely on camels for transportation. Camels carry people and goods throughout the Sahara.

Camels are perfectly suited to the harsh desert climate. They can go for long periods without water. When water is available, they are able to drink 25 percent of their body weight at one time. Camels do not sweat as much as other animals, so they do not lose much water in hot climates.

A camel's thick coat provides **insulation** and protects the animal from the hot and cold temperatures of the desert.

Sahara Desert Timeline

Prehistoric

65 million years ago
Dinosaurs become extinct.

120,000 years ago
Modern humans evolve.

7,000 years ago Nomads first arrive in the Sahara.

4,000 years ago The Sahara starts to become a desert.

2,700 years ago Arid conditions take over the Sahara region.

2,000 years ago
Camels are introduced to the Sahara.

Early Explorers

19 BC–AD 86 Romans explore the Sahara in a series of expeditions.

1798 Friederich Hornemann is the first European to cross the northeastern part of the Sahara.

1826 Alexander Gordon Laing is the first European to cross the Sahara to get to the city of Timbuktu. He dies on the return trip.

1828 René-August Caillié becomes the first European to return from a trip to Timbuktu.

Development

1880 European countries begin to lay claim to parts of Africa.

1955 A **civil war** begins in the Sudan.

1956 Morocco and Tunisia gain independence from France.

1960 France's first nuclear test is held in the Sahara Desert.

1962 Algeria gains independence from France.

1963 The Tuareg people begin the first rebellion against the government of Mali. The rebellion ends later the same year.

1983 The second civil war begins in the Sudan.

1990 The second Tuareg rebellion begins.

1996 The rebellion by the Tuareg ends.

Present

2001 The first "Festival in the Desert" is held in Mali.

2009 Nigeria, Algeria, and Niger sign an agreement to allow the world's longest pipeline to be built through the Sahara Desert.

2010 Universities in Algeria and Japan plan to build a silica manufacturing plant in the Sahara. It will process the silica found in sand to make solar panels.

Desertification

Every year, the Sahara gets a bit larger. It is estimated that it grows at least 3 to 6 miles (5 to 10 km) per year. This growth is caused by a process called desertification. Desertification occurs when desert begins to take over parts of the land that were once fertile. Sand and barren land replace the trees and other plants that once grew in the area. Desertification occurs because of natural events and human activities.

Natural events causing desertification are mainly climate related. Winds increase the size of the desert by blowing sand into areas where it is not normally found. Changes in the amount of rainfall and length of the wet season can also extend the range of a desert by reducing the amount of moisture the area receives.

Chinguetti was a small town founded in the 12th century. Once an important trade center, today it is covered in sand due to desertification.

Human actions also cause desertification. Trees in areas near deserts are cut down for personal use and to build homes. Without trees, the sands of the desert move into these areas and settle. As a result, the desert expands. Poor farming practices contribute to the problem. Some farmers allow their animals to feed on one part of the land too often and for too long. This is called overgrazing. Farmers may also plant their crops in one place over and over again. Both of these farming techniques take nutrients from the soil and invite a desert environment to drift in.

Should people be allowed to farm near the Sahara?

Yes	No
Farms supply the African population with the food they need to survive.	Crops can be grown in parts of Africa that are not as fragile.
Farming helps some people make a living.	Other industries can be developed that do not endanger the land as much as farming.
Farming does not have to destroy land. If people use farming practices that save the land, the problem will not be as widespread. People need to be shown how to use the land correctly.	The land is still at risk due to climate change. Farming adds to the problem, whether the land is used correctly or not.

Travel across the Desert

Years ago, people relied on camel caravans to cross the desert. For almost 2,000 years, camels were used to transport people and goods. Today, they are still used by nomadic groups, such as the Tuareg. However, many people now travel in trucks that are specially designed for the desert.

Traveling across the desert can be dangerous. There are large sections that are not populated. People who become lost or encounter problems may wait for days before they are found.

The desert environment can be very hard on people. It is hot during the day, cold at night, and there is usually very little food or water. Many travelers have been fooled by mirages. They think they see water in the distance, but it is really just a reflection of the sky. The sky shimmers in the distance on very hot days, which makes it look like water.

To avoid becoming stuck in the sand, people driving through the Sahara will often follow the tire tracks of other vehicles. These vehicles have already packed down the sand, making it safer for travel.

Oasis

The underground water source for an oasis may be located up to 500 miles (805 km) away.

An oasis is a place in the desert where underground water comes to the surface. An oasis is usually surrounded by **fertile** land. Plants such as figs, wheat, and citrus fruits grow in the oases of the Sahara.

Oases cover only 800 square miles (2,100 sq. km) of the Sahara Desert. About 75 percent of the Sahara's people live in or near these oases. The nomadic people use oases as they have for centuries—as places to rest and stock up on food and water.

Desert Stories

The peoples of the Sahara have many stories about the desert and their way of life. Most of these traditional stories are not written down. Instead, they are passed along **orally** from generation to generation.

In some parts of Africa, stories are told by people called griots. Griots play an important role in society. They are not only storytellers, but entertainers, poets, and historians as well. Griots learn about the past from their **ancestors**. They then pass the stories and history along to other generations. They accompany their stories with music and are often skilled musicians.

The traditional role of griots was to preserve the history and traditions of their people. Today, griots are most well known for their role as entertainers. However, they sometimes also serve as diplomats and advisors to their communities.

Festival in the Desert

For many years, the Tuareg have had gatherings in the desert. During these celebrations, thousands of nomads get together to race camels, share stories, and listen to music.

Today, one of the biggest festivals in the region is the Festival in the Desert. Held in various venues, the festival is a celebration of the music and culture of the Tuareg. It attracts musicians and tourists from all over the world.

About 30 performing arts groups from around the world are invited to participate in the Festival in the Desert each year.

What Have You Learned?

True or False?

Decide whether the following statements are true or false. If the statement is false, make it true.

1. Temperatures can reach 122°F (50°C) in the Sahara.

2. Alexander Gordon Laing was the first European to come back from Timbuktu alive.

3. The majority of the Sahara is covered by gravel plains called regs.

4. More than 300 species of migratory birds spend time in the Sahara.

5. Camels have thin coats to keep them cool.

6. West African storytellers are called griots.

Short Answer

Answer the following questions using information from the book.

1. Name four desert features.

2. Between which two latitudes are the trade winds found?

3. What are the Tuareg people also called?

4. In which year did Caillié reach Timbuktu?

5. Name five countries in the Sahara.

Multiple Choice

Choose the best answer for the following questions.

1. Which kind of animal is best suited for travel across the desert?
   a. horse
   b. camel
   c. goat

2. The name "Sahara" comes from the Arabic meaning what?
   a. desert
   b. very hot
   c. sand dune

3. What is an oasis?
   a. a mirage
   b. a type of camel
   c. a place where underground water comes to the surface

4. How much of the desert is covered by sand dunes?
   a. 30 percent
   b. 80 percent
   c. 15 percent

Activity

Build a Solar Still

People have found many ways to survive in the desert. For example, people use solar stills to gather water. Try building a solar still in your backyard.

Materials

1 jar

8 to 10 medium-sized rocks

1 measuring glass

1 smaller rock

1 clear garbage bag

1 shovel

Instructions

1. With the help of an adult, dig a round hole in a sandbox or garden. The hole must have a flat bottom and should be no bigger than a garbage bag. It must be deeper than the jar is tall.

2. Put the jar in the center of the hole.

3. Lay the garbage bag over the top of the hole. Put the medium-sized rocks on the edges of the bag to hold it in place.

4. Place the small rock in the center of the bag over the jar, and wait for the jar to fill with water.

Results

Over time, moisture from the ground and heat from the Sun causes condensation to form on the underside of the bag. The rock in the center of the bag directs the water to run into the jar. Use a measuring glass to find out how much water you collected.

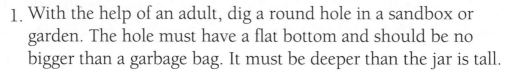

Key Words

adapt: to adjust to the environment

ancestors: relatives who came before the current generation

archaeologists: scientists who study past people and cultures

Berbers: a nomadic group of people found throughout northern Africa

civil war: fighting between groups from the same country

climate: weather conditions, including wind, rain, and temperature

crustaceans: mainly aquatic animals that have an outer shell covering their body

equator: an imaginary line that divides the world into a northern and southern half

expeditions: organized trips taken by a group of people

fertile: capable of producing plants

fossils: bones or other traces of plants or animals that have turned into stone

insulation: protection against heat, sound, or electricity

latitudes: imaginary lines that indicate the distance from the equator

mammals: a group of animals that include humans

migratory: moving from place to place, depending on the season

nomads: people who move from place to place with no permanent home

orally: spoken, instead of written

plateaus: flat, raised areas of land

precipitation: rain, snow, sleet, or hail that falls to the ground

reptiles: cold-blooded animals with tough, dry skin

Index

Log on to www.av2books.com

AV² by Weigl brings you media enhanced books that support active learning. Go to www.av2books.com, and enter the special code found on page 2 of this book. You will gain access to enriched and enhanced content that supplements and complements this book. Content includes video, audio, weblinks, quizzes, a slide show, and activities.

AV² Online Navigation

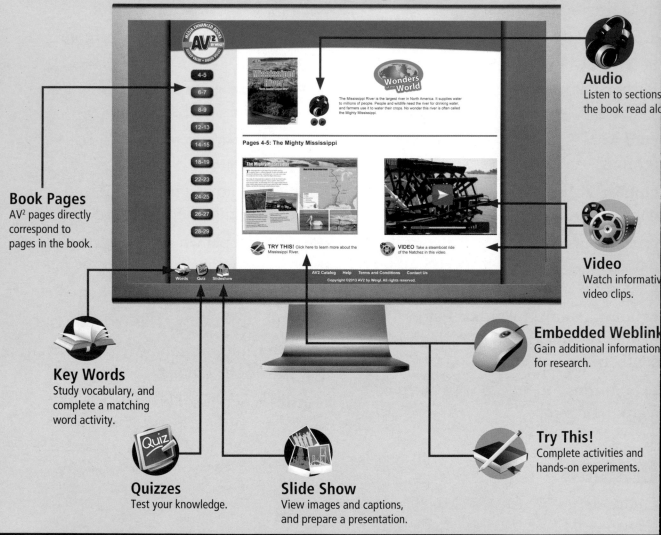

Book Pages
AV² pages directly correspond to pages in the book.

Key Words
Study vocabulary, and complete a matching word activity.

Quizzes
Test your knowledge.

Slide Show
View images and captions, and prepare a presentation.

Audio
Listen to sections the book read alo

Video
Watch informativ video clips.

Embedded Weblink
Gain additional information for research.

Try This!
Complete activities and hands-on experiments.

AV² was built to bridge the gap between print and digital. We encourage you to tell us what you like and what you want to see in the future.

Sign up to be an AV² Ambassador at www.av2books.com/ambassador.